Pl
Bal

GREAT
MOMENTS
&
DUBIOUS
ACHIEVEMENTS
IN BASEBALL
HISTORY

•

JOHN S. SNYDER

CHRONICLE BOOKS

SAN FRANCISCO

Printed in Singapore.

ISBN 0-8118-0038-5

Library of Congress Cataloging in Publication Data available.

Distributed in Canada by Raincoast Books, 112 East Third Avenue, Vancouver, B.C. V5T 1C8

10   9   8   7   6   5   4

Chronicle Books
275 Fifth Street
San Francisco, CA 94103

Introduction

Nearly 14,000 individuals have made their way into a big league base- ball game since the National League was established in 1876. Major league record books single out numerous players for achievements, recognizing them as the only player to accomplish a certain feat, placing them above all others or, in some cases, below all others. Many of the publicity-gen- erating records have been created by the elite, such as Babe Ruth, Ty Cobb, Pete Rose, Hank Aaron, and Joe DiMaggio. But baseball's unique bent on record keeping and the egalitarian nature of the sport have allowed several to cash in on everlasting fame with one great moment—or with one huge gaffe.

Don Larsen, a journeyman pitcher with an 81-91 lifetime record will be forever known for his perfect game in the 1956 World Series, the only post-season no-hitter ever. Johnny Vander Meer, another hurler with a career losing record, set a standard yet to be equalled with back-to-back no-hitters with the 1938 Cincinnati Reds. It is Johnny Burnett, a utility infielder with the Cleveland Indians in 1932, who holds the all-time mark for most hits in a game, not Rose or Cobb. Prestigious home run records are held by the likes of Tony Cloninger, Willie Aikens and Rudy York. Tom Cheney, winner of just 19 big league games, is the only one to fan 21 batters in a game, a figure that has eluded Nolan Ryan, Walter Johnson, Sandy Koufax and Roger Clemens.

The ignoble are also "honored" in this book, as baseball has been meticulous in its efforts in keeping records for most errors, most defeats and lowest batting average, among countless others.

Play Ball: Great Moments and Dubious Achievements in Baseball History is a journey through time, not only honoring those who have established records but also bringing them to life by capturing the stories behind the lines in the record books. Collected here are not dry statistics but untold stories of the many men who have risen above, or fallen below, all the others. After more than a century of baseball, each of these players is still *the only player* to accomplish each of these remarkable feats.

Hank Aaron

THE ONLY HITTER to collect more than 6,800 career total bases.

Aaron is best known as the all-time home run leader with 755, passing Babe Ruth's record of 714 amid national fanfare on April 8, 1974. Aaron also passed Ruth as the career runs-batted-in leader early in 1975, and finished his baseball days with 2,297, surpassing "The Babe's" figure of 2,211. But the most remarkable of Aaron's career records occurred in September 1972 and received scant media attention: "Hammerin' Hank" passed Stan Musial as the all-time leader in total bases. Musial's total base record stood at 6,134, and Aaron shattered that mark by finishing up in 1976 with 6,856.

Babe Adams

THE ONLY ROOKIE pitcher to win three World Series games.

Adams was a 27-year-old rookie with the Pittsburgh Pirates in 1909 and compiled a 12-3 record and a 1.11 earned run average. He still did not figure to be a large factor in the World Series against the Detroit Tigers because the Pirates had a "Big Three" of Vic Willis, Howie Camnitz, and Lefty Leifield, who combined for a 66-25 record during the year. Adams was the surprise choice of manager Fred Clarke, however, to be the starting pitcher in the first game, and he responded with a 4-1 win. With the series tied, he won game five 8-4, then the seventh 8-0. [Note: A pitcher is a rookie until pitching 50 career innings.]

Willie Aikens

THE ONLY PLAYER with multiple home run games in the same World Series.

He was born Willie Mays Aikens on October 14, 1954, just 12 days after Willie Mays led the New York Giants to a world championship with a spectacular catch in the World Series. Mays hit 660 regular season homers, the third best in history, but in 71 of his World Series at bats failed to hit a single home run. Aikens hit just 110 regular season homers in an eight-year career, but for the Kansas City Royals in the 1980 World Series against Philadelphia, he hit two homers in game one and two more in game four, the only time a player has had multiple home run games in a Series.

Dale Alexander

THE ONLY PLAYER to win an American League batting title playing for two different teams.

Alexander began the 1932 season with the Detroit Tigers, but by June 12 he had only 16 at bats and 4 base hits. He was traded that day to the Boston Red Sox and was immediately established as the everyday Boston first baseman. Alexander proceeded to win the batting title with a .367 average. Under today's rules, however, Alexander would not have been awarded the title. In 1932 a player needed to play in 100 games to qualify, and Alexander appeared in 124. But under the rules in force since 1957, Alexander would need 477 plate appearances; in 1932 he had only 453.

Charlie Babb

THE ONLY SHORTSTOP to commit five errors in a nine-inning game twice in his career.

There have been only four instances since 1900 in which a shortstop has been charged with five errors in a game, and Babb was responsible for two of those four. The first was with the New York Giants on August 24, 1903, the second with the Brooklyn Dodgers on June 20, 1904. Babb played only three years in the majors and hit .243 with no home runs.

Neal Ball

THE ONLY PLAYER to hit a home run and to pull off an unassisted triple play in the same game.

Both feats also came in the same inning. It was the first home run of Ball's career, the only one he hit in 1909, and one of only four he hit in a seven-year career. And it was the first unassisted triple play in major league history. Ball was playing shortstop for the Cleveland Indians against the Boston Red Sox on July 19, 1909. In the second inning, with Cy Young pitching, Heinie Wagner on second, and Jake Stahl on first, Ball caught Amby McConnell's line drive, stepped on second to retire Wagner, and tagged Stahl, who was running on the play, coming into second base. The Indians won the game 6-1.

Hank Bauer

THE ONLY PLAYER to hit safely in 17 consecutive World Series games.

Bauer played in 53 World Series games for the New York Yankees between 1949 and 1958 and hit just .245, but set a record with a 17-game hitting streak. He hit safely in all seven games in 1956 against the Brooklyn Dodgers, each of the seven contests in 1957 versus the Milwaukee Braves, and the first three in 1958 before being stopped by Milwaukee's Warren Spahn. During the streak, Bauer hit .316. In the 17th game of the hitting streak, Bauer became the only player to drive in all four runs of a World Series contest. He had a two-run single and a two-run homer in a 4-0 Yankee win.

George Bell

THE ONLY PLAYER to hit three
home runs in an Opening Day game.

The 1987 American League Most Valuable
Player started the 1988 season with three
home runs on Opening Day to lead the
Toronto Blue Jays to a 5-3 win over the
Royals in Kansas City. All three homers
were hit off Bret Saberhagen.

Bill Bergen

THE ONLY HITTER with as many as 2,500 career at bats to hit as low as .170.

Bergen is the worst hitter in history by a wide margin. Playing catcher for the Cincinnati Reds between 1901 and 1903 and the Brooklyn Dodgers between 1904 and 1911, Bergen's season batting averages were .179, .180, .227, .182, .190, .159, .159, .175, .139, .161, and .132. His weak hitting was not offset by great power or any ability to reach base on balls. Bergen hit only two home runs and coaxed only 88 walks out of pitchers in his 11 seasons.

Bill Bevens

THE ONLY PITCHER in World Series history to lose a one-hitter.

Bevens started game four of the 1947 World Series for the New York Yankees against the Brooklyn Dodgers at Ebbets Field. The Yankees led 2-1, with the Dodgers scoring on two walks and a throwing error. With two out in the ninth, Bevens still had a no-hitter. Carl Furillo of the Dodgers walked. Al Gionfriddo ran for Furillo and stole second. Bevens intentionally walked Pete Reiser, his 10th walk of the game, still a Series record. Eddie Miksis ran for Reiser. Cookie Lavagetto, a pinch-hitter, doubled and Gionfriddo and Miksis came around to score. The Dodgers won 3-2.

Babe Birrer

THE ONLY PLAYER to collect all six of his career runs-batted-in in one game.

Birrer, who pitched in 56 games with the Tigers, Orioles, and Dodgers between 1955 and 1958, collected his only six career runs-batted-in while playing for Detroit on July 19, 1955. Birrer pitched four innings of shutout relief against Baltimore, hit a pair of three-run homers in his only two at bats, and was the winning pitcher in a 12-4 decision.

Max Bishop

THE ONLY PLAYER to draw eight walks in a double header.

Bishop drew eight walks in a double header twice in his career. Playing second base for the Philadelphia Athletics, Bishop had eight walks on May 21, 1930, in 15-7 and 4-1 wins over the New York Yankees, despite Babe Ruth's three home runs in the first game. With the Red Sox on July 8, 1934, Bishop drew eight bases on balls in 7-4 and 7-2 victories over the Athletics in Boston. Bishop had more walks than base hits five seasons during his career. And he had one walk per every 3.9 at bats during his career, the second-best figure in history behind Ted Williams.

Ray Boggs

THE ONLY PITCHER to hit three batters with pitches in his first inning in
the majors.

Only 12 pitchers in major league history
have hit three batters in an inning, and
Boggs is the only one to do it in his first
inning in the majors. Pitching for the
Boston Braves on September 17, 1928,
Boggs pitched the ninth and hit three batters, issued two walks, and threw a wild
pitch. Amazingly, the Chicago Cubs scored
only one run in the inning, but still came
away with a 15-5 win.

Bobby Bonds

THE ONLY PLAYER with over 300 career home runs and over 400 lifetime stolen bases.

In his 14-year major league career, Bonds hit 332 home runs and swiped 461 bases. The well-traveled Bonds played for the Giants, Yankees, Angels, White Sox, Rangers, Indians, Cardinals, and Cubs. He had 30 or more home runs and 30 or more stolen bases in five different seasons.

Jim Bottomley

THE ONLY PLAYER to drive in 12 runs in a single game.

Bottomley drove in his 12 runs playing first base for the St. Louis Cardinals on September 16, 1924, in a 17-3 win over the Dodgers at Ebbets Field in Brooklyn. He had six hits in six at bats with a two-run single in the first, a run-scoring double in the second, a grand slam homer in the fourth, a two-run homer in the sixth, a two-run single in the seventh, and a run-scoring single in the ninth. Bottomley had 111 or more runs-batted-in six seasons in a row beginning in 1924, and led the league twice.

Roger Bresnahan

THE ONLY MANAGER to watch his club surrender 10 runs before a batter was retired.

Bresnahan was not only the manager of the St. Louis Cardinals on May 13, 1911, when the New York Giants scored 10 times without a man being retired, but he was also the catcher. At the end of the first inning, the Giants led 13-0, and Bresnahan wisely took himself out of the lineup, and New York manager John McGraw removed starting pitcher Christy Mathewson to save his ace for a closer ball game. Rube Marqaurd pitched the final eight innings for the Giants and struck out 14 batters, which still stands as the National League record for most strikeouts by a relief pitcher in one game. New York won 19-3.

Ken Brett

THE ONLY PITCHER to hit a home run in four consecutive games.

Brett struck home runs in four straight starting assignments with the 1973 Philadelphia Phillies, on June 9, 13, 18, and 23. He also was the winning pitcher in all four games. Brett played 14 years in the majors with the Red Sox, Brewers, Phillies, Pirates, Yankees, White Sox, Angels, Twins, Dodgers, and Royals, finishing his pitching career 83-85 and hitting .262 with 10 home runs in 347 at bats.

Grant Briggs

THE ONLY MAJOR league catcher to allow 19 opposing runners to steal a base in one game.

As a rookie with Syracuse of the American Association, on April 22, 1890, Briggs allowed 19 Philadelphia runners to steal a base in a 17-6 loss.

Buster Brown

THE ONLY PITCHER to lose two-thirds of his decisions.

Brown holds the record for the lowest winning percentage with a minimum of 150 decisions for his 51-105 record (.327) with the St. Louis Cardinals, Philadelphia Phillies, and Boston Braves between 1905 and 1913. He died on February 9, 1914, of blood poisoning following an operation for the removal of a growth under his right arm.

Three-Finger Brown

THE ONLY PITCHER to complete at least 20 games and save 13 others in a single season.

Mordecai Peter Centennial Brown was the ace starter and ace reliever of the Chicago Cubs in 1911. He had a 21-11 record with 21 complete games in 27 starts, and in 26 relief appearances was 5-3 with 13 saves. It was the sixth consecutive year in which Brown won at least 20 games. But the double duty took its toll. In 1912, Brown was 5-6 and was 11-12 with the Cincinnati Reds in 1913.

Johnny Burnett

THE ONLY PLAYER to collect nine hits in a major league game.

In one of the most amazing performances in baseball history, Burnett had seven singles and two doubles for the Cleveland Indians in an 18-inning game on July 10, 1932, against the Philadelphia Athletics. No other major league player has had more than seven hits in one game. Burnett's nine hits, which came in 11 at bats, were in a losing cause. The Athletics, behind six hits and three homers by Jimmie Foxx, won 18-17.

Ray Caldwell

THE ONLY PITCHER to hit pinch-hit home runs in consecutive at bats.

Caldwell was a 133-120 pitcher between 1920 and 1921, with a .248 lifetime batting average that was bolstered by frequent pinch-hit appearances. On June 10 and 11, 1915, he became the first player in major league history to homer in consecutive pinch-hit at bats. On June 12, in a game he pitched, Caldwell homered again to give the New York Yankees a 9-5 win over the St. Louis Browns. Despite homers in three straight days, Caldwell hit only four in 1915 and just eight in his career.

Ed Cartwright

THE ONLY MAJOR leaguer to drive in seven runs in one inning.

Playing first base for St. Louis of the American Association against Philadelphia on September 23, 1890, Cartwright drove in seven runs on a three-run homer and a grand slam in an eleven-run third inning. St. Louis led 21-2 when the contest was called after seven innings by darkness.

Bob Caruthers

THE ONLY PITCHER with a winning percentage over .690.

Caruthers pitched for Brooklyn and St. Louis clubs in both the American Association and the National League between 1884 and 1892 and compiled a 218-97 won-lost record. The .692 winning percentage remains the best for more than 200 victories. And pitching was not even his primary position. Caruthers played 366 games in the outfield, 340 as a pitcher, 13 at first base, and 9 at second. His lifetime batting average was .282.

Joe Cassidy

THE ONLY ROOKIE in American League history to hit 19 triples in a season.

Cassidy belted 19 triples for the Washington Senators in 1904, despite only a .241 batting average. The next season, Cassidy's production slipped to four triples and a .215 average. The young shortstop died on March 25, 1906, less than two months after his 23rd birthday. Wire service reports two days after his death stated that Cassidy had been ill for "several weeks with a peculiar disease, which his doctors termed purpuro hemorrhagia, the blood turning to water. A number of specialists, however, disagreed with the diagnosis."

Frank Chance

THE ONLY MANAGER to guide his club to 116 wins in a season.

Chance's 1906 Chicago Cubs had a 116-36 record, including victories in 55 of their last 65 games. In the World Series, the Cubs faced their crosstown rival White Sox, a club known as the "Hitless Wonders" because of their .230 season batting average. In the only all-Chicago World Series in history, the White Sox stunned the Cubs four games to two. Player-manager Chance and the Cubs came back to capture the world championship from the Detroit Tigers in both 1907 and 1908, the only two World Series ever won by the Cubs.

Tom Cheney

THE ONLY PITCHER to fan over 20 batters in a major league game.

Roger Clemens is recognized as the single-game strikeout leader because of the 20 he fanned for the Boston Red Sox in a nine-inning game against the Seattle Mariners in 1986. But the record for a complete game is held by Tom Cheney, who in 16 innings with the Washington Senators on September 12, 1962, struck out 21 Baltimore Orioles. Cheney, a pitcher with a 19-29 lifetime record, had 13 strikeouts after nine innings and rang up victim number 21 in the 16th. The Senators won the game in Baltimore 2-1 on a home run by Bud Zipfel.

Fred Clarke

THE ONLY MANAGER to watch his
team allow 36 runs in one game.

Clarke was only 24 when he became manager of the Louisville Colonels in 1897 and,
in one of his first games as skipper, saw his
club lose 36-7 to the Chicago Cubs, the all-
time record for runs scored by one club in
a game. By direct contrast, Clarke is also
the only big league manager to watch his
club pitch shutouts in six consecutive
games, when he was with the Pittsburgh
Pirates in June 1903. Clarke played 21
seasons in the majors and hit .315 with
2,708 hits. He managed 19 seasons, won
four National League pennants in
Pittsburgh, and was elected to the Hall of
Fame in 1945.

Jack Clements

THE ONLY LEFT-HANDED catcher to play more than 1,000 games at the position.

Left-handed catchers are an extreme rarity, but Clements played 1,073 games behind the plate in 17 seasons in the majors, between 1884 and 1900, mostly with the Philadelphia Phillies. He had a .286 lifetime batting average and in 1895 hit .394.

Tony Cloninger

THE ONLY PITCHER to hit two grand slam home runs in one game.

Not only is Cloninger the only pitcher to hit two grand slams in one game, he is also the only pitcher to hit two slams ever. The Atlanta Braves pitcher had his big day, July 3, 1966, at the expense of the San Francisco Giants at Candlestick Park. The grand slams came in the first and fourth innings. He is also the only National League player to hit two grand slams in a single game. Less than three weeks earlier, Cloninger had hit two homers in a June 16 game against the Mets in Atlanta.

Ty Cobb

THE ONLY PLAYER to collect six hits in six at bats and hit three home runs in the same game.

Cobb pulled off the feat on May 5, 1925, to lead the Detroit Tigers to a 14-8 win over the St. Louis Browns. Cobb also had two doubles. The next day, he had two home runs in an 11-4 victory over St. Louis to become the only player between 1884 and 1936 to hit five homers in consecutive games.

Eddie Collins

THE ONLY PLAYER since 1900 to
steal six bases in one game.

   Collins twice performed the feat of six
steals, and he did it in the span of 11 days.
On September 11, 1912, as second base-
man with the Philadelphia Athletics,
Collins stole six on rookie catcher Brad
Kocher in a 9-7 win over the Detroit Tigers.
On September 22, he deep-sixed the St.
Louis Browns with another six steals in an
8-2 victory.

Jimmy Cooney

THE ONLY PLAYER to be involved in
two unassisted triple plays.

Of the only eight unassisted triple plays,
Cooney was a part of two, once as a
baserunner and once as a fielder. On May
7, 1925, playing for the Cardinals against
the Pirates, Cooney was on second, Rogers
Hornsby on first, and Jim Bottomley at bat.
Bottomley lined to shortstop Glenn Wright,
who stepped on second to retire Cooney
and tagged out Hornsby. On May 30, 1927,
Cooney was playing shortstop for the Cubs,
again against the Pirates. In the fourth inning, with Lloyd Waner on second, Clyde
Barnhart on first, and Paul Waner at bat,
Cooney caught Waner's liner, stepped on
second, and tagged the running
Barnhart.

Sam Crawford

THE ONLY PLAYER to hit more than 300 career triples.

Crawford's career, which began in 1899 and ended in 1917, was during the days of pasture-sized playing fields and a dead ball. He hit 312 triples, leading the league six times, but had only 97 lifetime home runs. He had 2,964 career hits and a .309 average.

Tony Cuccinello

THE ONLY PLAYER to lose a batting title by less than a thousandth of a point.

Cuccinello lost the closest batting race in major league history in 1945 by hitting .30845 for the Chicago White Sox, .00009 behind the New York Yankees' Snuffy Stirnweiss, who batted .30854. He played 16 years in the majors and had a career batting average of .280 in 1,704 games.

Joe Cunningham

THE ONLY PLAYER to hit three home runs in his first two major league games.

In his debut on June 30, 1954, with the St. Louis Cardinals, Cunningham homered in an 11-3 win over the Reds in Cincinnati. The next day, he hit two home runs off Warren Spahn in a 9-2 victory against the Milwaukee Braves. In his first seven at bats Cunningham batted-in nine runs. He lasted 12 years in the majors as a first baseman and outfielder with the Cardinals, White Sox, and Senators, hitting .291 and 64 homers.

Willie Davis

THE ONLY PLAYER to make three errors in one inning in a World Series game.

Davis played center field for the Los Angeles Dodgers against the Baltimore Orioles in 1966. In the fifth inning of game two, with the score 0-0, one out, and Boog Powell on first base, Paul Blair lifted a fly ball to Davis, who dropped it for a two-base error. Powell stopped at third. Andy Etchebarren followed Blair to the plate and hit a short fly ball to Davis. Davis dropped it, then threw wildly past third base for another error in an attempt to retire Blair. Both Powell and Blair scored, and Etchebarren came around on a Luis Aparicio double. The Orioles won 6-0.

Ed Delahanty

THE ONLY PLAYER with a four home run game and a four double game in his career.

Eleven players share an all-time record for four home runs in a game and 36 have a record for four doubles in a game, but Delahanty is the only one to accomplish both feats. A .345 lifetime hitter, fourth best of all time, Delahanty hit four homers on July 13, 1896, although his Phillies lost 9-8 to Chicago. He had four doubles for Philadelphia on May 13, 1899, in a 9-0 win over New York.

Rick Dempsey

THE ONLY PLAYER to win a 1-0 game lasting more than 20 innings by hitting a home run.

Dempsey set the record for the latest home run to win a 1-0 game on August 23, 1989, to give the Los Angeles Dodgers a victory over the Expos in Montreal. It is the second longest 1-0 game in major league annals. The blast was surrendered in the 22nd inning by Dennis Martinez, normally a starter, but who was pressed into a relief role for the first time in three years.

Joe DiMaggio

THE ONLY MAJOR leaguer to reach base in 74 consecutive games.

DiMaggio thrilled the baseball world in his 1941 season with the New York Yankees by collecting a base hit in a record 56 consecutive games from May 15 through July 16. His hitting streak was stopped on July 17 by Cleveland Indian pitchers Al Smith and Jim Bagby, but DiMaggio did draw a walk to reach base for the 57th straight game. He collected a hit in each of his next 17 games to extend his streak to 74. The streak ended on August 3 when Johnny Niggeling of the St. Louis Browns prevented DiMaggio from reaching base in four plate appearances.

Moe Drabowsky

THE ONLY RELIEF pitcher to strike out 11 batters in a World Series game.

When the 1966 season began, Drabowsky was a 30-year-old pitcher with a 48-81 lifetime record on four clubs. He was best known as the pitcher who gave up Stan Musial's 3,000th career hit in 1958 and as the losing pitcher when Early Wynn won his 300th career game in 1963. Drabowsky was 6-0 with the Orioles in 1966, however, and had a sensational day in the World Series against the Los Angeles Dodgers. He entered the first game with one out in the third inning, and went the rest of the way allowing no runs, one hit, and striking out 11, including 6 in a row. The Orioles won 5-2, then completed the sweep.

Roberto Clemente

THE ONLY PLAYER to finish a career with exactly 3,000 hits.

Clemente became the 11th player in history to reach the coveted 3,000 hit mark on September 30, 1972, with a double off Jon Matlack of the Mets. The Pittsburgh Pirate great never collected another regular season hit because on December 31, 1972, he died in a plane crash in the waters off the coast of his native Puerto Rico carrying supplies for earthquake victims in Nicaragua.

Hugh Duffy

THE ONLY MAJOR leaguer to hit over .435 in a season.

Duffy set the major league record for batting average in a season in 1894 with Boston in the National League by hitting .438. He also led the league in home runs, runs-batted-in, hits, slugging average, and total bases. Duffy had a career average of .328 and was elected to the Hall of Fame in 1945.

Bill Duggleby

THE ONLY PLAYER to hit a grand slam in his first at bat.

Duggleby debuted with the Phillies on April 21, 1898, and opened with a grand slam off Cy Seymour of the New York Giants in a 13-4 Philadelphia win. Duggleby had a total of six major league homers and a 92-104 won-lost record in eight seasons.

Leo Durocher

THE ONLY PLAYER to circle the
bases on a bunt in All-Star competition.

Although he hit only .217 for the Brooklyn
Dodgers in 1938, Durocher was the starting shortstop for the National League in the
annual All-Star Game, played in
Cincinnati. In the eighth inning, with the
Nationals leading 2-1 and Frank
McCormick on first base, Durocher
directed a sacrifice bunt toward third baseman Jimmie Foxx. Foxx threw Durocher's
bunt past first base. Joe DiMaggio, playing
out of position in right field, overthrew
home plate trying to prevent McCormick
from scoring, and Durocher circled the
bases on a "bunt home run." The Nationals
won 4-1.

Terry Felton

THE ONLY PITCHER to lose each of
his 16 major league decisions.

Playing for the Minnesota Twins, Felton
was 0-3 in 1980 and 0-13 in 1982. He also
holds the record for most losses in a season without a win. It made no difference
whether Felton came out of the bullpen or
was used as a starter. He was 0-9 in relief
and 0-7 in a starting role. His final career
earned run average was 5.53.

Wes Ferrell

THE ONLY PITCHER to hit 38 career home runs.

Ferrell is also the only pitcher to hit nine home runs in a season, which occurred in 1931. He is also the only pitcher to give up a home run to his brother and hit a home run himself in the same game. It happened on July 19, 1933, with Wes pitching for the Cleveland Indians and his brother Rick catching for the Boston Red Sox at Fenway Park. In the top of the fourth inning, with Rick calling the pitches, Wes hit a home run. In the bottom of the fourth, Rick homered off Wes. Rick Ferrell was elected to the Hall of Fame in 1984. Wes Ferrell is still waiting for a plaque at Cooperstown, despite a 193-128 career record.

Whitey Ford

THE ONLY PITCHER to allow 13
runs in All-Star competition.

Ford's regular season winning percentage
of .690 with the New York Yankees is the
highest of any pitcher after 1900, his 10
World Series victories are the best of all
time, and his 33 consecutive innings of
shutout ball in World Series play are also a
record. But in the All-Star Game, Ford was
a disaster. In six games, he pitched 12 innings, allowed 19 hits and 13 runs, 11 of
which were earned, and lost his only two
decisions. Ford was elected to the Hall of
Fame in 1974, with a 236-106 record for
11 Yankee pennant winners. He pitched at
least 200 innings in each season; in all but
one he had a higher winning percentage
than the Yankee ball club.

Jimmie Foxx

THE ONLY PLAYER to hit 500 career
home runs before his 33rd birthday.

Foxx was 32 years, 11 months, and 2
days old when he hit home run number
500 while playing for the Boston Red Sox
on September 24, 1940, against the Philadelphia Athletics. The next youngest to hit
500 home runs was Willie Mays, at 34
years, 4 months, and 7 days. Babe Ruth
and Henry Aaron were also 34 when they
reached the 500 home run plateau. Despite
hitting 500 home runs at a younger age
than anyone else by more than a year, Foxx
finished his career with 534 and has been
passed on the all-time list by eight players.

Paul Foytack

THE ONLY PITCHER to allow home runs to four consecutive batters.

With the Los Angeles Angels on July 31, 1963, in an encounter with the Cleveland Indians, Foytack was belted four times in succession by Woodie Held, Pedro Ramos, Tito Francona, and Larry Brown. Foytack's blowup happened in the sixth inning of a 9-5 Cleveland win.

George Frazier

THE ONLY RELIEF pitcher to lose three games in a World Series.

Frazier had an 0-1 record in 16 games during the regular season with the New York Yankees in 1981, and won a game against the Oakland A's in the League Championship Series, but was 0-3 in the World Series versus the Los Angeles Dodgers. In game three, Frazier came on in the fourth inning with New York leading 4-3. He gave up two runs, and the Dodgers won 5-4. The next day, Frazier surrendered two runs in the seventh with the score tied 6-6, and the Yankees lost 8-7. In the sixth and final game, Frazier was blasted for three runs in the fifth. The Dodgers won 9-2.

Gary Gaetti

THE ONLY PLAYER to start two triple plays in one game.

The Minnesota Twins, on July 17, 1990, against the Boston Red Sox at Fenway Park, became the only club in major league history to complete two triple plays in one game. Gaetti, at third base, started both of them. With runners on first and second, he twice fielded a hot grounder, stepping on third and throwing to second baseman Al Newman, who in turn fired to Kent Hrbek at first. The batting victims were Tom Brunansky in the fourth inning and Jody Reed in the eighth. The Red Sox still won the game 1-0.

Alexander Gardner

THE ONLY CATCHER to allow 12 passed balls in a single game.

Gardner played in only one major league game but managed to put himself in the record books with a still-standing, and probably unsurpassable, record of 12 passed balls in a game. He played for Washington in the American Association on May 10, 1884, in an 11-3 loss to New York.

Lou Gehrig

THE ONLY PLAYER to hit 14 home runs against a single opponent in one season.

Gehrig hit a career-high 49 home runs in 1936 and picked on Cleveland Indians pitching for 14 of them, hitting 6 in 11 games at Yankee Stadium and 8 in 12 games at Cleveland. The Yankees won 16 games, lost 6, and tied 1 against the Indians that season.

Bill George

THE ONLY PITCHER to walk 13 or more batters in a game three times in a career.

George walked 13 batters in a game three times within a 29-day span. No other pitcher in history has ever walked more than 13 in a game more than once. George did this in 1887 when the pitcher's mound was just 50 feet from home plate and it took five balls to issue a walk. The four-ball count was not instituted until 1889, and the pitching rubber was not set at 60 feet, 6 inches until 1893. George walked 13 while performing for the New York Giants against Indianapolis on May 15, 1887, 16 on May 30 versus Chicago, and 13 against Indianapolis on June 15.

Bob Gibson

THE ONLY PITCHER to win seven
consecutive World Series starts.

Gibson not only won all seven, but each
was a complete game. He lost his first
World Series contest in game two in 1964
to the Yankees by an 8-3 score. In game
five, Gibson gave the Cardinals a 5-2 win
and clinched the world championship with
a 7-5 victory in game seven. In 1967 versus
the Red Sox, Gibson won game one 2-1,
game four 6-0, and the seventh and deciding contest 7-2. In 1968 against the Tigers,
Gibson opened the series with a 4-0 win in
which he struck out a record 17 batters.
Gibson won the fourth game 10-1, but
ended the winning streak in the seventh
game with a 4-1 loss.

Fred Gladding

THE ONLY HITTER with at least 50 at bats and a batting average under .020.

Gladding had a 48-34 record and 109 saves with the Detroit Tigers and Houston Astros between 1961 and 1973, but with a bat in his hands he was hopeless. His one base hit in 63 at bats came on July 30, 1969, off Ron Taylor of the New York Mets in the ninth inning, in which Houston scored 11 runs and became one of only five clubs in history to hit two grand slam homers in a single inning.

Lefty Gomez

THE ONLY PITCHER with six World Series wins without a loss.

Gomez's 6-0 World Series mark is the best perfect record in the history of the Fall Classic. Gomez was 1-0 for the New York Yankees in 1932, 2-0 in 1936, 2-0 in 1937, and 1-0 in 1938. He also had a no decision in a start in 1939. Gomez's World Series earned run average was 2.86, and in his seven starts, the Yankees averaged 8.8 runs per game. In the regular season, Gomez was 189-102 and was elected to the Hall of Fame in 1972.

Dwight Gooden

THE ONLY PLAYER to lead the league in a major statistical category at the age of 19 years, 10 months, and 14 days.

Gooden is the youngest pitcher to lead the National League in strikeouts, a record he earned in 1984 as a rookie with the Mets. By the end of the season, he had fanned 276 batters in 218 innings. Gooden is also the youngest to lead the league in earned run average, wins, complete games, and innings pitched, which he accomplished in 1985 as a 20-year-old.

Billy Goodman

THE ONLY UTILITY player to win a batting title.

Goodman won the American League batting title in 1950 with a .354 average for the Boston Red Sox while playing 45 games in the outfield, 27 at third base, 21 at first, 5 at second base, and 1 at shortstop. Except for a few games in 1950 filling in for third baseman Johnny Pesky, Goodman remained on the bench until Ted Williams broke his elbow in the All-Star Game. Goodman became the regular left fielder in Williams's absence and accumulated enough at bats for the batting title.

Peaches Graham

THE ONLY PITCHER to be victimized by a no-hitter in his only major league pitching appearance.

Graham played seven years in the majors, mostly as a catcher, but at one time or another performed at all nine positions. The only time he took the mound was on September 18, 1903, with the Chicago Cubs, and opposing pitcher Chick Fraser of the Philadelphia Phillies pitched a no-hitter for a 10-0 win.

Ray Grimes

THE ONLY PLAYER in history to
drive in runs in over 15 consecutive
games.

Among all of the great run producers in
baseball history, the record for most consecutive games driving in at least one run
belongs to the relatively obscure Ray
Grimes. With the Chicago Cubs in 1922,
Grimes drove in 27 runs in 17 contests between June 27 and July 23. In all, he drove
in 99 runs that season in 138 games and
had a .354 batting average.

Bob Groom

THE ONLY PITCHER to throw 11 innings in one day without allowing a single hit.

Pitching for the St. Louis Browns against the Chicago White Sox on May 6, 1917, Groom came in to pitch the final two innings of the first game of a double header and allowed no hits. Groom started the second game and threw a nine-inning complete-game no-hitter to win 3-0. Even though this was early in the season, it was already the sixth no-hitter pitched in the majors in 1917.

Lefty Grove

THE ONLY PITCHER to lead his
league in earned run average nine
times.

Grove led the American League in earned
run average nine times with the Philadelphia Athletics and Boston Red Sox between
1926 and 1939. No one else has ever been
an ERA leader more than five seasons in a
career. Grove was 300-141 lifetime, and his
winning percentage of .680 is the best in
history by any pitcher with at least 350 decisions. He was elected to the Hall of Fame
in 1947.

Cesar Gutierrez

THE ONLY PLAYER to collect seven hits in seven at bats in an American League game.

Gutierrez had only 128 base hits in his major league career for a .235 average, but on June 21, 1970, playing shortstop for the Detroit Tigers, he looked like Ty Cobb. Cesar had six singles and a double as the Tigers downed the Cleveland Indians 9-8 in 12 innings. Three of Cesar's seven hits in the game never left the infield. Gutierrez also wore uniform number seven, and in 1971, his last year in the majors, he had only seven hits all season.

Harvey Haddix

THE ONLY PITCHER to carry a perfect game beyond nine innings.

With the Pittsburgh Pirates on May 26, 1959, against the Braves in Milwaukee, Haddix retired all 36 hitters through the first 12 innings. Milwaukee pitcher Lew Burdette scattered 12 Pirate hits in tossing 13 innings. In the bottom of the 13th, the Braves broke up the perfect game by a score of 1-0. It was a crushing defeat for Haddix, who pitched one of the best games in history. He was 12-12 during the 1959 season and was 136-113 during his career, which lasted through 1965.

Art Hagan

THE ONLY PITCHER in major league history to lose a game by the score of 28-0.

Hagan was on the mound the entire game for Philadelphia on August 21, 1883, in a 28-0 defeat to Providence, the most lopsided shutout in major league annals. To make matters worse, Providence was Hagan's hometown. He lasted only two years in the major leagues and retired with a won-lost record of 2-18.

Odell Hale

THE ONLY MAJOR leaguer to start a triple play with his forehead.

Hale was playing third base for the Cleveland Indians on September 7, 1935, with his club leading the Boston Red Sox 5-3. With the bases loaded and none out in the ninth inning, batter Joe Cronin hit a vicious liner at Hale, which glanced off his glove, hit him on the forehead, and deflected to shortstop Bill Knickerbocker without the ball hitting the ground. Knickerbocker quickly threw the ball to second baseman Roy Hughes to force Billy Werber, and Hughes tossed to first baseman Hal Trosky to retire Mel Almada, complete the triple play, and end the game.

Ron Hansen

THE ONLY PLAYER to pull off an unassisted triple play, hit a grand slam,
and be traded in a span of 72 hours.

Hansen had a busy few days in 1968. On
July 30, playing shortstop for the Washington Senators against the Cleveland
Indians, he completed the only unassisted
triple play in the majors since 1927.
Hansen fielded a line drive, stepped on second to double off the runner, and tagged
another runner going into the base. The
Senators lost 10-1. On August 1, Hansen
broke a string of six consecutive strikeouts
by hitting a grand slam home run against
the Tigers. On August 2, he was traded to
the Chicago White Sox.

Mel Harder

THE ONLY PITCHER to throw 13 innings in All-Star competition without allowing a run.

Harden pitched 13 scoreless innings for the American League in four appearances between 1934 and 1937. He was 72-50 during those four seasons and 223-186 in his career, which lasted from 1928 to 1947, and was spent with the Cleveland Indians.

Carroll Hardy

THE ONLY PLAYER to pinch-hit for Ted Williams.

Hardy was baseball's "pinch-hitter of the rich and famous." In 1958, while with the Cleveland Indians, Hardy pinch-hit for Roger Maris and hit a three-run homer to win the game. In 1960, with the Red Sox, Hardy was on the bench when Ted Williams fouled a pitch off his foot and had to be removed from the game. Hardy completed the at bat. And, in 1961, he was used as a pinch-hitter for a young rookie named Carl Yastrzemski.

Jack Harper

THE ONLY PLAYER to play on both the team with the most losses and the team with the most wins.

As a rookie in 1899, Harper pitched for the Cleveland Spiders, which lost a major league record 134 games while winning only 20. In his last season, in 1906, Harper pitched one game for the Chicago Cubs, which set a big league standard for wins with a 116-36 record.

Joe Harris

THE ONLY PITCHER in history to
hurl 24 innings in a game, and lose.

No one has ever had to go so far to lose a
game. Pitching for the Boston Red Sox on
September 1, 1906, against the Philadelphia Athletics, Harris was on the wrong
end of a 4-1 score after pitching a 24-in-
ning complete game. Harris was a pitcher
who could have used a break. In 1906, he
had a 2-21 record and pitched eight games
in which his Boston teammates failed to
score a run. In his three-year career, Harris
was 3-30.

Billy Hatcher

THE ONLY PLAYER to hit .750 in a World Series.

Hatcher placed his name into the record book with a superlative World Series in 1990, leading the Cincinnati Reds to a four-game sweep of the Oakland Athletics. With nine hits, including four doubles and a triple, in 12 at bats, he hit .750 to break Babe Ruth's record of .625 set in 1928.

Dwight Gooden

THE ONLY PLAYER to lead the league in a major statistical category at the age of 19 years, 10 months, and 14 days.

Gooden is the youngest pitcher to lead the National League in strikeouts, a record he earned in 1984 as a rookie with the Mets. By the end of the season, he had fanned 276 batters in 218 innings. Gooden is also the youngest to lead the league in earned run average, wins, complete games, and innings pitched, which he accomplished in 1985 as a 20-year-old.

Billy Goodman

THE ONLY UTILITY player to win a batting title.

Goodman won the American League batting title in 1950 with a .354 average for the Boston Red Sox while playing 45 games in the outfield, 27 at third base, 21 at first, 5 at second base, and 1 at shortstop. Except for a few games in 1950 filling in for third baseman Johnny Pesky, Goodman remained on the bench until Ted Williams broke his elbow in the All-Star Game. Goodman became the regular left fielder in Williams's absence and accumulated enough at bats for the batting title.

Peaches Graham

THE ONLY PITCHER to be victimized by a no-hitter in his only major league pitching appearance.

Graham played seven years in the majors, mostly as a catcher, but at one time or another performed at all nine positions. The only time he took the mound was on September 18, 1903, with the Chicago Cubs, and opposing pitcher Chick Fraser of the Philadelphia Phillies pitched a no-hitter for a 10-0 win.

Ray Grimes

THE ONLY PLAYER in history to drive in runs in over 15 consecutive games.

Among all of the great run producers in baseball history, the record for most consecutive games driving in at least one run belongs to the relatively obscure Ray Grimes. With the Chicago Cubs in 1922, Grimes drove in 27 runs in 17 contests between June 27 and July 23. In all, he drove in 99 runs that season in 138 games and had a .354 batting average.

Bob Groom

THE ONLY PITCHER to throw 11 innings in one day without allowing a single hit.

Pitching for the St. Louis Browns against the Chicago White Sox on May 6, 1917, Groom came in to pitch the final two innings of the first game of a double header and allowed no hits. Groom started the second game and threw a nine-inning complete-game no-hitter to win 3-0. Even though this was early in the season, it was already the sixth no-hitter pitched in the majors in 1917.

Lefty Grove

THE ONLY PITCHER to lead his league in earned run average nine times.

Grove led the American League in earned run average nine times with the Philadelphia Athletics and Boston Red Sox between 1926 and 1939. No one else has ever been an ERA leader more than five seasons in a career. Grove was 300-141 lifetime, and his winning percentage of .680 is the best in history by any pitcher with at least 350 decisions. He was elected to the Hall of Fame in 1947.

Cesar Gutierrez

THE ONLY PLAYER to collect seven hits in seven at bats in an American League game.

Gutierrez had only 128 base hits in his major league career for a .235 average, but on June 21, 1970, playing shortstop for the Detroit Tigers, he looked like Ty Cobb. Cesar had six singles and a double as the Tigers downed the Cleveland Indians 9-8 in 12 innings. Three of Cesar's seven hits in the game never left the infield. Gutierrez also wore uniform number seven, and in 1971, his last year in the majors, he had only seven hits all season.

Harvey Haddix

THE ONLY PITCHER to carry a perfect game beyond nine innings.

With the Pittsburgh Pirates on May 26, 1959, against the Braves in Milwaukee, Haddix retired all 36 hitters through the first 12 innings. Milwaukee pitcher Lew Burdette scattered 12 Pirate hits in tossing 13 innings. In the bottom of the 13th, the Braves broke up the perfect game by a score of 1-0. It was a crushing defeat for Haddix, who pitched one of the best games in history. He was 12-12 during the 1959 season and was 136-113 during his career, which lasted through 1965.

Art Hagan

THE ONLY PITCHER in major league history to lose a game by the score of 28-0.

Hagan was on the mound the entire game for Philadelphia on August 21, 1883, in a 28-0 defeat to Providence, the most lopsided shutout in major league annals. To make matters worse, Providence was Hagan's hometown. He lasted only two years in the major leagues and retired with a won-lost record of 2-18.

Odell Hale

THE ONLY MAJOR leaguer to start a
triple play with his forehead.

Hale was playing third base for the Cleveland Indians on September 7, 1935, with
his club leading the Boston Red Sox 5-3.
With the bases loaded and none out in the
ninth inning, batter Joe Cronin hit a
vicious liner at Hale, which glanced off his
glove, hit him on the forehead, and
deflected to shortstop Bill Knickerbocker
without the ball hitting the ground.
Knickerbocker quickly threw the ball to
second baseman Roy Hughes to force Billy
Werber, and Hughes tossed to first baseman Hal Trosky to retire Mel Almada, complete the triple play, and end the game.

Ron Hansen

THE ONLY PLAYER to pull off an un-assisted triple play, hit a grand slam, and be traded in a span of 72 hours.

Hansen had a busy few days in 1968. On July 30, playing shortstop for the Washing-ton Senators against the Cleveland Indians, he completed the only unassisted triple play in the majors since 1927. Hansen fielded a line drive, stepped on sec-ond to double off the runner, and tagged another runner going into the base. The Senators lost 10-1. On August 1, Hansen broke a string of six consecutive strikeouts by hitting a grand slam home run against the Tigers. On August 2, he was traded to the Chicago White Sox.

Mel Harder

THE ONLY PITCHER to throw 13 innings in All-Star competition without allowing a run.

Harden pitched 13 scoreless innings for the American League in four appearances between 1934 and 1937. He was 72-50 during those four seasons and 223-186 in his career, which lasted from 1928 to 1947, and was spent with the Cleveland Indians.

Carroll Hardy

THE ONLY PLAYER to pinch-hit for Ted Williams.

Hardy was baseball's "pinch-hitter of the rich and famous." In 1958, while with the Cleveland Indians, Hardy pinch-hit for Roger Maris and hit a three-run homer to win the game. In 1960, with the Red Sox, Hardy was on the bench when Ted Williams fouled a pitch off his foot and had to be removed from the game. Hardy completed the at bat. And, in 1961, he was used as a pinch-hitter for a young rookie named Carl Yastrzemski.

Jack Harper

THE ONLY PLAYER to play on both the team with the most losses and the team with the most wins.

As a rookie in 1899, Harper pitched for the Cleveland Spiders, which lost a major league record 134 games while winning only 20. In his last season, in 1906, Harper pitched one game for the Chicago Cubs, which set a big league standard for wins with a 116-36 record.

Joe Harris

THE ONLY PITCHER in history to hurl 24 innings in a game, and lose.

No one has ever had to go so far to lose a game. Pitching for the Boston Red Sox on September 1, 1906, against the Philadelphia Athletics, Harris was on the wrong end of a 4-1 score after pitching a 24-inning complete game. Harris was a pitcher who could have used a break. In 1906, he had a 2-21 record and pitched eight games in which his Boston teammates failed to score a run. In his three-year career, Harris was 3-30.

Billy Hatcher

THE ONLY PLAYER to hit .750 in a World Series.

Hatcher placed his name into the record book with a superlative World Series in 1990, leading the Cincinnati Reds to a four-game sweep of the Oakland Athletics. With nine hits, including four doubles and a triple, in 12 at bats, he hit .750 to break Babe Ruth's record of .625 set in 1928.

Duster Mails

THE ONLY PITCHER with more than 15 career innings in the World Series without giving up a run.

Mails appeared in only one World Series during his career and was spectacular with 15 2/3 shutout innings for the 1920 Cleveland Indians against the Brooklyn Dodgers. He pitched 6 2/3 innings of scoreless relief in game two and a shutout on three hits in game six against the Dodgers. Mails had a 14-7 record for the Indians in 1921, but faded to 4-7 in 1922, his last year in Cleveland. He spent two years in the minors before resurfacing with the St. Louis Cardinals in 1925 and 1926, then was out of the majors for good with a 32-25 career record.

Jim Maloney

THE ONLY PITCHER to throw two extra-inning no-hitters.

There have been 14 extra-inning no-hitters in major league baseball, 7 of which have lasted 10 innings or more, and Maloney has accounted for 2 of those, both in 1965. With the Cincinnati Reds on June 14, 1965, against the New York Mets, Maloney pitched 10 innings of no-hit ball before a lead-off homer in the 11th gave the Mets a 1-0 win at Cincinnati. On August 19 against the Cubs in Chicago, Maloney had another nine-inning no-hitter go into extra innings. Cincinnati shortstop Leo Cardenas homered in the top of the 10th to give the Reds a 1-0 lead, and Maloney held the Cubs hitless in the bottom half.

Connie Mack

THE ONLY INDIVIDUAL to manage clubs more than 50 years in the major leagues.

Mack managed the Pittsburgh Pirates for 3 years, from 1894 through 1896, and the Philadelphia Athletics for 50 remarkable years, beginning in 1901. Born during the Civil War, Mack was still managing in the majors during the Korean conflict at the age of 87. The next oldest manager was Casey Stengel at 74. Mack always seemed to be at the top or the bottom of the American League standings. In his years in Philadelphia, Mack finished first nine times and second seven, but was dead last for 17 seasons.

Red Lucas

THE ONLY PITCHER with over 60 pinch-hits.

Lucas gained his greatest fame as a pinch-hitter. His 114 career pinch-hits are not only the best by a pitcher by a wide margin, but are the fifth best of all-time. Lucas held the major league record for most career pinch-hits from 1933 until 1965. He finished with a .281 lifetime batting average.

Mickey Lolich

THE ONLY PLAYER to hit his only career home run in a World Series game.

Lolich, a pitcher with a .110 batting average, had no home runs over 16 seasons. But in the second game of the 1968 World Series, Lolich homered off Nelson Briles of the St. Louis Cardinals to lead the Detroit Tigers to an 8-1 win. Lolich did more than that in the World Series: he pitched three complete game victories, including one over Bob Gibson in game seven to clinch the world championship for Detroit. Lolich had a 217-191 lifetime record as a pitcher.

Freddie Lindstrom

THE ONLY 18-YEAR-OLD to play in a World Series.

During the regular season in 1924, Lindstrom batted only 79 times, hit .253, and played just 11 games at third base for the New York Giants. But in the World Series against the Washington Senators, Lindstrom started every game at third in place of the injured Heinie Groh and was the Giants lead-off hitter in each of the seven contests. Lindstrom responded to the pressure with 10 hits and a .333 batting average.

Don Lenhardt

THE ONLY PLAYER to hit grand slams for two different clubs in a span of seven days.

Lenhardt hit a grand slam for the Red Sox on June 2, 1952, his second bases-clearing blast of the season, but the very next day was traded to the Detroit Tigers in a nine-player deal. On June 9, he hit another grand slam against his former Boston teammates.

Bill LeFebvre

THE ONLY PLAYER to hit a home run in the only at bat of his first year in the majors.

Debuting on June 10, 1938, with the Boston Red Sox as a pitcher, LeFebvre hit a home run in his first big league at bat. He also allowed six runs in four innings of a 15-2 loss to the Chicago White Sox. It was the only game LeFebvre pitched that season. He played in 74 more big league games with the 1939 Red Sox and the 1943 and 1944 Washington Senators. Although he failed to hit another home run, he had a .276 lifetime average and led the American League in pinch-hits in 1944.

Tony Lazzeri!

THE ONLY PLAYER to drive in 15 runs in consecutive games.

In the second game of a double header on May 23, 1936, Lazzeri hit two home runs good for four runs-batted-in to lead the New York Yankees to a 15-1 thrashing of the Philadelphia Athletics. The next day, he became the first player in history to stroke two grand slam home runs in one game. He also hit a third homer with no one on base and a two-run triple. The 11 runs-batted-in set an American League record, which still stands, as the Yankees defeated the Athletics 25-2.

Don Larsen

THE ONLY PITCHER to throw a no-hitter in a World Series game.

Larsen not only pitched the only no-hitter in World Series history, but tossed a perfect game as well. He pulled off the improbable feat on October 8, 1956, for the New York Yankees in the fifth game against the Brooklyn Dodgers. The Yankees won 2-0. As a result of this performance, he is the best example of a mediocre player becoming famous for one extraordinary game. Larsen had a career record of 81-91 and was just 55-68 as a starting pitcher. His record at the time he tossed his no-hitter was 30-38. His erratic pitching continued until he left the majors in 1967.

Jack Lapp

THE ONLY CATCHER to throw out
five base runners in a World Series
game.

Lapp was a back-up catcher for most of
his nine-year career. Playing in 1911 with
the Philadelphia Athletics, he was behind
the plate in only 57 regular season games
and in just 2 of 6 World Series contests
against the New York Giants. But in the
third game, on October 17, five Giant base
runners attempted to steal, and Lapp
nailed every one of them; he also threw out
Fred Snodgrass trying to advance from second to third on a passed ball.

Harvey Kuenn

THE ONLY PLAYER who was the final out in a no-hitter twice by the same pitcher.

Kuenn was the final out in two of the four no-hitters pitched by Sandy Koufax. On May 11, 1963, while with the San Francisco Giants, Kuenn bounced out to Koufax to end the no-hitter and clinch an 8-0 Los Angeles Dodger victory. On September 9, 1965, as a member of the Chicago Cubs, Kuenn was the 27th batter and 27th out in Koufax's perfect game. Kuenn had a 15-year career in the majors with a .303 batting average and 2,092 hits. In 1982, he was the manager of the American League champion Milwaukee Brewers.

Sandy Koufax

THE ONLY PLAYER in history to strike out in 12 consecutive plate appearances.

Not only did Koufax strike out 12 times in a row, but they were the first 12 at bats of his career and his only at bats in 1955 as a Brooklyn Dodger. During his career, Koufax had 75 hits in 776 at bats for an .097 average. It was Koufax's arm, not his bat, that brought him into the Hall of Fame in 1972, the youngest ever elected. Yet he is the only pitcher to lead the league in earned run average five consecutive seasons, which he accomplished between 1962 and 1966 with marks of 2.54, 1.88, 1.74, 2.04, and 1.73.

Jim Konstanty

THE ONLY PITCHER to start a World Series game after making no starts during the regular season.

Philadelphia Phillies manager Eddie Sawyer entered the 1950 World Series against the New York Yankees with a short-handed pitching staff due to injuries and the Army. Ace starter Robin Roberts had been used three days earlier to clinch the pennant, so Sawyer settled on Konstanty to start the first game. In his World Series start, Konstanty pitched eight innings and allowed only one run and four hits, but the Phillies lost 1-0. He won the National League Most Valuable Player Award for his excellent work in 74 games in relief in which he was 16-7 with 22 saves.

Malachi Kittridge

THE ONLY MANAGER to lose the first 13 games of the season in his first year as manager.

Kittridge was a catcher in the majors for 16 seasons and had a .219 batting average, the second worst in history by anyone with at least 4,000 at bats. Given the opportunity to manage the 1904 Washington Senators, Kittridge lost his first 13 games. After its first victory of the season, Washington lost three more games, and Kittridge was relieved of his duties and ended his managerial career with a 1-16 record.

Bruce Kison

THE ONLY PITCHER in League Championship play to win four games without a defeat.

Kison's perfect won-lost record in the history of the League Championship Series was earned in four different series. With the Pittsburgh Pirates in 1971, Kison won the fourth and deciding game against the San Francisco Giants in relief. He had another relief win against the Cincinnati Reds in the third game in 1972. Kison started game three versus the Los Angeles Dodgers in 1974, and was the only Pirate pitcher to best Los Angeles in that series. And in 1982, Kison started and won game three for the California Angels against the Milwaukee Brewers.

Al Mamaux

THE ONLY PITCHER to give up 10
runs in the 13th inning of a game.

In one of the weirdest pitching performances of all time, Mamaux pitched 12
shutout innings for the Brooklyn Dodgers
against the Cincinnati Reds on May 15,
1919, then fell apart and gave up 10 runs
in the 13th to lose 10-0. Mamaux also had
a strange career. He was 21-8 as a 21 year
old for his hometown Pittsburgh Pirates in
1915, and was 21-15 in 1916. In 1917,
however, he was 2-11 with a 5.25 earned
run average. Mamaux finished his 12-year
career in 1924 at 76-67.

Mickey Mantle

THE ONLY PLAYER to homer in a World Series at the age of 20 years, 11 months, and 16 days.

Mantle became the youngest hitter to homer in a World Series game on October 6, 1952, against the Dodgers in Brooklyn in a 3-2 Yankee win. By 1964, Mantle had a World Series record 18 home runs. He is the youngest ever to hit a homer in a World Series game by only seven days, however. On October 5, 1957, Tony Kubek, Mantle's Yankee teammate, hit two homers against the Braves in his home town of Milwaukee at the age of 20 years, 11 months, and 23 days.

Roger Maris

THE ONLY PLAYER to hit over 50 home runs in a season while batting less than .270.

Maris set a major league record in 1961 with 61 home runs for the New York Yankees, but hit just .269. A 50-home-run season has been accomplished 17 times in major league history by 10 different players. The highest batting average by a player with 50 home runs was Babe Ruth's .378 in 1921, when he clouted 59 homers.

Pepper Martin

THE ONLY PLAYER with more than 50 World Series at bats and a higher than .400 batting average.

Martin was a rookie outfielder for the St. Louis Cardinals in 1931 who electrified the nation with his hustling play in the World Series against the Philadelphia Athletics. He had 12 hits in 24 at bats and five stolen bases to lead his club to a world championship. As a participant in three World Series, Martin had 23 hits, including 7 doubles, a triple, and a homer, in 55 at bats, plus 14 runs scored and 7 stolen bases, for a batting average of .418.

Jim Mason

THE ONLY PLAYER to hit a home run in his only World Series at bat.

Mason, a back-up shortstop for the New York Yankees in 1976, entered game three of the World Series against the Cincinnati Reds after Fred Stanley was lifted for a pinch-hitter. In his only at bat, in the seventh inning, Mason homered off Pat Zachry into the left field stands at Yankee Stadium. In a nine-year, 633-game big league career, Mason hit only .203 with just 12 home runs.

Charlie Maxwell

THE ONLY PLAYER to hit five extra-inning home runs in a season.

Maxwell was "Mr. Clutch" in 1960 when he hit 5 of his 24 home runs for the Detroit Tigers in extra innings. He also specialized in hitting home runs in unusual combinations. A total of 40 of his 148 career home runs were hit on Sundays, and 12 of those were against the New York Yankees. The most memorable came on May 3, 1959, when Maxwell hit home runs in four consecutive at bats as the Tigers swept the Yankees in a double header. Maxwell had eight runs-batted-in in the 4-2 and 8-2 triumphs.

Willie Mays

THE ONLY PLAYER with four home runs in one game and three triples in another.

Mays is one of only 11 players in major league history with four home runs in a game and is the only one of those to hit three triples in a game during his career. The four homer game came on April 30, 1961, to give the San Francisco Giants a 14-4 win over the Braves at County Stadium in Milwaukee. He had three triples on September 15, 1960, in an 8-6, 11-inning win over the Philadelphia Phillies. Mays is also the youngest player ever to collect 50 home runs in a season, which he accomplished in 1955 when he clouted 52 for the New York Giants at the age of 24.

Jim McAndrew

THE ONLY PITCHER to suffer four consecutive shutout losses.

Not only is McAndrew the only pitcher to lose four shutouts in a row, but they were his first four major league decisions and he allowed only six runs. On July 21, 1968, in St. Louis, McAndrew and the New York Mets lost 2-0 to Bob Gibson and the Cardinals. On August 4, he was defeated 2-0 by Mike Kekich and the Dodgers in Los Angeles. Loss number three came on August 10 with a 1-0 win by the Giants and Bobby Bolin in San Francisco. And, on August 17, he lost 1-0 to Don Wilson and the Houston Astros at Shea Stadium. On August 26 he had his first major league victory, a 1-0 triumph over Steve Carlton and the Cardinals.

Joe McCarthy

THE ONLY MANAGER since 1900 with 1,000 games to maintain a winning percentage of over .600.

McCarthy managed 24 years in the majors, beginning in 1926 with the Cubs, then going to the Yankees and Red Sox. In his career he had a winning percentage of .614, won nine pennants and seven world championships, and had a World Series record of 30-13, a winning percentage of .698. McCarthy never won a close pennant race. Each of his nine winners was won by nine games or more. Five of the clubs he managed lost the pennant by four games or fewer.

Jack McCloskey

THE ONLY MANAGER to lose a game because his club ran out of baseballs.

McCloskey's Louisville Colonels started the game against the Brooklyn Dodgers on May 23, 1895, with only three baseballs, and two of those were practice balls borrowed from the Dodgers. A messenger was sent across town for a new supply, but the streetcar the messenger was traveling on broke down and the three original balls were worn beyond use by the third inning. The game was awarded to Brooklyn since it is the responsibility of the home team to supply balls.

Willie McCovey

THE ONLY PLAYER to win a Rookie of the Year award with less than two months experience in the major leagues.

McCovey began the 1959 campaign with Phoenix in the Pacific Coast League and batted .372 with 29 home runs and 92 runs-batted-in in 95 games. Called up to the San Francisco Giants on July 30, he went 4-for-4 in his first game, including 2 triples, and in 52 games hit .354 with 13 homers and 38 RBIs. Not only did McCovey capture the National League Rookie of the Year Award, but he was the unanimous choice of the 24-member selection commit-tee chosen by the Baseball Writers' Associ-ation of America.

Joe McGinnity

THE ONLY PITCHER to win two complete games in one day three times in his career.

Not only is McGinnity the only pitcher to perform the feat, but he did it in the span of one month. Pitching for the New York Giants, on August 1, 1903, he beat the Braves 4-1 and 5-2, on August 8 defeated the Brooklyn Dodgers 6-1 and 4-3, and on August 31 downed the Philadelphia Phillies 4-1 and 9-2. During the 1903 campaign, McGinnity was 31-20, on his way to a 247-144 career.

John McGraw

THE ONLY MANAGER to win 26 consecutive games.

McGraw's New York Giants won 26 games in succession from September 7 through September 30, 1916. He is also the only manager to guide a club through two winning streaks of 15 games or more in the same season, as the 1916 Giants also had a 17-game winning streak in May of that year. Despite the two long winning streaks, the club finished in fourth place with an 86-66 record.

Bill McGunnigle

THE ONLY MANAGER to lose five games in two days.

McGunnigle's Louisville club lost all three games in the second of only three triple headers in major league history, played in Baltimore on September 7, 1896, by scores of 4-3, 9-1, and 12-1. The following day, Louisville dropped two more to Baltimore, 10-9 and 3-1. Louisville finished the season in 1ast place in the 12-team National League, 53 games behind the pennant-winning Orioles.

Johnny Mize

THE ONLY PLAYER to hit three home runs in a game six times.

Mize's team won only one of the games. His first three-home-run game was July 13, 1938, with the St. Louis Cardinals, but the Boston Braves won 10-5. Seven days later, Mize had three homers in a 7-1 Cardinal win over the Giants. On May 13, 1940, Mize hit three in Cincinnati, but the Reds and Cardinals tied 8-8 in a game called by darkness. His three homers on September 8, 1940, came in a 16-14 loss to the Pirates. While with the Giants, Mize hit three against the Boston Braves on April 24, 1947, but the Giants lost 14-5. And on September 15, 1950, Mize hit three for the Yankees in a 9-7 loss to the Tigers.

Terry Moore

THE ONLY PLAYER with 10 All-Star Game at bats without a base hit.

Moore, one of the best defensive outfielders of his day, failed to hit in the All-Star Game. Representing the St. Louis Cardinals in 1939, 1940, 1941, and 1942, Moore was hitless in 10 at bats, the largest collar in history. Moore had a .280 regular season average in 11 seasons.

Guy Morton

THE ONLY PITCHER to lose his first 13 major league decisions and still finish his career with a winning record.

Morton, nicknamed "The Alabama Blossom," started his career with the Cleveland Indians in 1914 with an 0-13 record, but finished up in 1924 at 98-88.

Manny Mota

THE ONLY PLAYER to collect 150 pinch-hits in a career.

Mota lasted 20 years in the majors, from 1962 through 1982, because of his ability to come off the bench and deliver a key hit. Playing with the New York Giants, Pittsburgh Pirates, Montreal Expos, and Los Angeles Dodgers, he had 150 pinch-hits in 505 official at bats, a .297 career pinch-hit average. Mota had a .304 career batting average in 1,536 games, but never played often enough in any one season to collect enough at bats to qualify for a batting title.

Stan Musial

THE ONLY PLAYER with more than 175 career triples and 175 home runs.

In his 22-year career with the St. Louis Cardinals, from 1941 through 1963, Musial had 177 triples and 475 home runs. He also had 725 doubles, third highest in history.

Greasy Neale

THE ONLY INDIVIDUAL to play in a World Series and coach in a Rose Bowl and a National Football League Championship game.

Neale played eight seasons in the major leagues from 1916 through 1924 and batted .259 as an outfielder with the Reds and Phillies, and starred in the 1919 World Series for Cincinnati by hitting .357. During the off-season, Neale coached football. He led an underdog Washington & Jefferson squad against powerful California in the 1922 Rose Bowl, and came away with a 0-0 tie. Neale later coached the Philadelphia Eagles, winning the NFL title in both 1948 and 1949 with shutouts in each of the championship games.

Hal Newhouser

THE ONLY PITCHER to win Most Valuable Player Award two years in a row.

Newhouser had a lifetime record of 34-52 entering the 1944 season, but came away with the MVP trophy after a 29-9 campaign for the Detroit Tigers. In 1945 the Tigers went to the World Series on the strength of Newhouser's 25-9 won-lost mark. In 1946 Newhouser nearly became the only player at any position to win MVP three years in a row, finishing second in the balloting with 197 points just behind Ted Williams's 224.

Bobo Newsom

THE ONLY PLAYER to change uni-
forms 16 times during his career.

Between 1929 and 1953, Newsom
pitched for the Brooklyn Dodgers
(1929–30), Chicago Cubs (1932), St. Louis
Browns (1934–35), Washington Senators
(1935–37), Boston Red Sox (1937), the
Browns again (1938–39), Detroit Tigers
(1939–41), the Senators again (1942), the
Dodgers again (1942–43), the Browns a
third time (1943), the Senators a third time
(1943), Philadelphia Athletics (1944–46),
the Senators a fourth time (1946–47), New
York Yankees (1947), New York Giants
(1948), the Senators a fifth time (1952),
and the Athletics again (1952–53). Newsom
was 20-16 with the Browns in 1938 with
a 5.08 earned run average.

Joe Niekro

THE ONLY PLAYER to hit his one big league home run off his brother.

Joe Niekro hit only one home run in his 22 seasons in the major leagues, and it came at the expense of his brother Phil. The incident occurred on May 29, 1976, and Joe's homer helped the Houston Astros to a 4-3 win over the Atlanta Braves.

Bob Nieman

THE ONLY PLAYER to hit home runs in his first two major league at bats.

In his debut with the St. Louis Browns on September 14, 1951, Nieman belted home runs in his first two at bats at Fenway Park. He also had a single, but the Boston Red Sox won 9-6. Nieman spent 12 years in the majors and hit .295 with 125 home runs, mostly as a platoon outfielder and pinch-hitter.

Les Nunamaker

THE ONLY CATCHER to throw out three base stealers in one inning.

On August 3, 1914, with the New York Yankees, Nunamaker became the first catcher since 1900 to perform the feat. In the first inning, Donie Bush, George Moriarty, and Hugh High of the Detroit Tigers all singled and attempted to steal a base, but Nunamaker threw them out one by one. A classic back-up catcher, he played 12 years in the majors in 715 games with a respectable .268 average on four clubs.

Joe Oeschger

THE ONLY PITCHER to hurl more than 20 consecutive shutout innings in one game.

In the longest game in major league history, on May 1, 1920, Oeschger pitched 21 straight scoreless innings for the Boston Braves in a 1-1 tie against the Brooklyn Dodgers. The game was called after 26 innings by darkness. The only run Oeschger allowed came in the fifth inning. His opposite number, Leon Cadore, pitched the entire game for the Dodgers, surrendering the lone Boston tally in the sixth. Oeschger and Cadore are the only pitchers ever to pitch 26 innings in one day, a record likely never to be broken.

Bill O'Hara

THE ONLY PLAYER to steal two bases in a game as a pinch-runner twice in his career.

There have been only nine instances in major league history in which a pinch-runner has stolen two bases in an inning, and O'Hara is the only one to do it twice—and in consecutive games. With the New York Giants, on September 1, 1909, he was inserted into the game as a pinch-runner in the sixth inning and stole second and third in a 9-6 win over the St. Louis Cardinals. The next day, O'Hara stole two, but St. Louis won 5-2.

Bill O'Neill

THE ONLY SHORTSTOP to commit six errors in one game.

While with the Boston Red Sox, O'Neill became the only shortstop since 1900 to make six errors in a single game, on May 21, 1904, against the St. Louis Browns. The Sox lost 5-3 in 13 innings. This was only O'Neill's second big league game at the position. He moved to the outfield and never played another game at short.

Mel Ott

THE ONLY PLAYER to score six runs in a game twice in a career.

Only five players since 1900 have accounted for six runs scored in a game, and Ott is the only one to do it twice. The first was on August 4, 1934, when Ott scored six times in a 21-4 New York Giants win over the Philadelphia Phillies. He reached base on two homers, a double, a single, a walk, and after being hit by a pitch. On April 30, 1944, he reached base on five walks and two singles, and scored six times in New York's 26-8 victory over the Brooklyn Dodgers. Ott is also the player to hit the most home runs in one ballpark. He connected for 323 of his career total 511 in the Polo Grounds in 22 seasons with the New York Giants.

Marv Owen

THE ONLY PLAYER to go hitless in
31 consecutive World Series at bats.

Owen played third base for the Detroit
Tigers in the World Series of 1934 and
1935. He collected only three hits in 49 at
bats for an .061 average and was hitless in
his final 31 at bats against the St. Louis
Cardinals in 1934 and the Chicago Cubs in
1935.

Ernie Padgett

THE ONLY PLAYER to complete an unassisted triple play in his first year in the majors.

Padgett completed the unaided triple play on his first day as a big league short-stop with the Boston Braves on October 6, 1923. In the second game of a double header, Walker Holke of the Philadelphia Phillies hit a liner to Padgett, who ran to second to retire Cotton Tierney and tagged Cliff Lee before he could return to first. Padgett played in 267 more big league games through 1927, but only 20 of them were at short.

Doc Parker

THE ONLY PITCHER to allow more than 20 runs in a National League game.

Parker had not pitched in the majors in five years when given a trial by the Cincinnati Reds on June 21, 1901, in a game against the Brooklyn Dodgers. He allowed 21 runs, the most by a National League pitcher since 1900, and 26 hits, and the Reds lost 21-3. "Next time I get in the box," said Parker after the game, "I hope to give a better account of myself." He never got another chance as that was his last big game. His career ended with a 5-8 record.

Joe Pate

THE ONLY PITCHER with nine wins and no defeats in his first big league season.

Pate had the best perfect record by any pitcher in big league history when he was 9-0, all in relief, with the 1926 Philadelphia Athletics. Unfortunately, Pate never won another big league game. He was 0-3 in 1927, his second and last season in the majors.

Roger Peckinpaugh

THE ONLY PLAYER to commit eight errors in a World Series.

Playing shortstop for the Washington Senators, Peckinpaugh was the American League Most Valuable Player in 1925. But in the World Series he was charged with eight errors as the Senators were dropped by the Pittsburgh Pirates in seven games. Peckinpaugh is also the youngest manager in history, guiding the Yankees for the final 17 games in 1914 at the age of 23.

Herb Pennock

THE ONLY PITCHER to win a game before his 20th birthday and a game after his 40th.

Pennock debuted with the Philadelphia Athletics in 1912 and won his first game at the age of 18. His final victory came as a 40-year-old with the Boston Red Sox in 1934. Pennock had a 240-162 lifetime record.

Lou Piniella

THE ONLY PLAYER to win a Rookie of the Year Award while playing for his third big league club.

Piniella debuted in the majors in 1964, playing in four games with the Baltimore Orioles. After spending time in the Washington Senators farm system, he performed in six games with the 1968 Cleveland Indians. In October 1968, he was selected by the Seattle Pilots in the expansion draft, and on April 1, 1969, was traded to the Kansas City Royals. Piniella hit .282 in 1969 for the Royals to win the American League Rookie of the Year Award. He lasted in the majors as a player until 1984, finishing with a .291 lifetime batting average and four World Series appearances with the New York Yankees.

Jack Quinn

THE ONLY PLAYER over age 45 to hit a home run since 1900.

A pitcher with the Philadelphia Athletics, Quinn homered just eight days short of his 46th birthday on June 27, 1930, off Chad Kimsey of the St. Louis Browns in an 8-3 win. It was one of only eight homers that Quinn hit in a 23-year career and was his first home run in 8 years. In the 1930 World Series, Quinn had a two-inning relief stint to become the oldest player ever to appear in the Fall Classic. When he was released by the Cincinnati Reds in July 1933, he was two days past his 49th birth-day, the oldest player in history who was not a part of a publicity stunt.

Dick Radatz

THE ONLY RELIEF pitcher to strike out over 180 batters in a single season.

Radatz was the best relief pitcher in baseball between 1962 and 1964 with the Boston Red Sox. He fanned 487 batters in 414 innings for an average of 10.59 strike-outs per nine innings. His season high was 181 strikeouts in 1964, the all-time record for relievers. He had a 40-21 record during those three seasons, coupled with 78 saves, and he won or saved 118 of the Red Sox's 224 victories. Radatz suddenly lost his touch after 1964. His record between 1965 and the end of his career in 1969 was 12-22.

Ed Reulbach

THE ONLY PITCHER to hurl two complete-game, nine-inning shutouts in one day.

Reulbach pitched the double shutout for the Chicago Cubs on September 26, 1908, with 5-0 and 3-0 wins over the Brooklyn Dodgers. The first game was a five-hitter, the second a three-hitter. The achievement could not have come in a more pressured situation. The Cubs were involved in a tight three-way pennant race with the Pittsburgh Pirates and New York Giants, and entered the day's action with only a half-game lead on both clubs. Chicago eventually captured first place, their third pennant in a row.

Jerry Reuss

THE ONLY PITCHER to lose seven League Championship Series games.

In the National League Championship Series, Reuss had an 0-7 record and a 5.45 earned run average. With the Pittsburgh Pirates, Reuss lost two in 1974 against the Los Angeles Dodgers and one in 1975 versus the Cincinnati Reds. As a member of the Dodgers, Reuss suffered one defeat in 1981 against the Montreal Expos, two in 1983 facing the Philadelphia Phillies, and one to the St. Louis Cardinals in 1985. When his career ended in 1990, Reuss had a record of 220-191.

Dusty Rhodes

THE ONLY PINCH-HITTER to drive in six runs in a World Series.

Rhodes had a fairy-tale World Series in 1954 for the New York Giants against the heavily favored Cleveland Indians. In the first game, Rhodes pinch-hit for Monte Irvin with one out in the 10th, the score 2-2, and two on base. His homer barely cleared the right field wall only 260 feet from home plate. Pinch-hitting for Irvin in the fifth inning of the second game, Rhodes's single tied the score 1-1. (He then replaced Irvin in left field and in the lineup and hit a seventh-inning homer to give the Giants a 3-1 win.) In game three, Rhodes batted for Irvin in the third inning and hit a two-run single. The Giants won in four straight.

Sam Rice

THE ONLY PLAYER to collect 200 hits in a season after his 40th birthday.

As an outfielder with the Washington Senators in 1930 at the age of 40, Rice had 207 hits and a .349 batting average. It was the sixth time in his career that he had a 200-hit season, and none came before he turned 30. Rice had 2,561 hits in all after his 30th birthday. Only Pete Rose had more. Rice gained a long overdue entry into the Hall of Fame in 1963.

Bobby Richardson

THE ONLY PLAYER to drive in six runs in a World Series game.

Richardson is also the only player to drive in 12 runs in a World Series. Both feats came in 1960 after a regular season in which he played 150 games for the New York Yankees and had just 1 homer and 26 runs-batted-in. He drove in two runs in game two and had his record-setting game in the third contest against the Pittsburgh Pirates. Richardson hit a grand slam in the first inning and a two-run single in the fourth. He batted in one more run in the fourth game and three in game six to give him a record twelve for the series.

Charlie Robertson

THE ONLY PITCHER to throw a no-hitter against a club with a team batting average of .305.

Not only did Robertson no-hit the 1922 Detroit Tigers, which had a composite average of .305, but he pitched a perfect game. It was only the third start of Robertson's career, which would end in 1928 with an inglorious record of 49-80. Pitching for the Chicago White Sox on April 30, 1922, Robertson retired nine times in a row, in order, a line-up that included player-manager Ty Cobb and Harry Heilmann. The Tigers were convinced that Robertson was using an illegal substance on the ball. The umpire allowed Cobb to frisk Robertson for evidence, but none was found.

Wilbert Robinson

THE ONLY MANAGER to go 58 innings in three consecutive games without a victory.

Robinson's frustration began on Saturday, May 1, 1920, when his Brooklyn Dodgers played a 26-inning 1-1 tie, the longest game in major league history, against the Braves in Boston. Since at the time Sunday ball was not permitted in Massachusetts, the Dodgers traveled back to Brooklyn to play the Philadelphia Phillies on May 2, and lost 4-3 in 13 innings. On Monday, May 3, the Dodgers went back to Boston, and lost to the Braves 2-1 in 19 innings. In three consecutive days, the Dodgers traveled from Boston to Brooklyn and back again, and suffered two losses and a tie.

Pete Rose

THE ONLY PLAYER to appear in more than 500 games at five different positions.

Rose was at first base in 939 games, at second base in 628, at third base in 634, in left field in 671, and in right field in 595. He is also the only player to play in five different positions in the All-Star Game, and in each one he was a starter. Rose was in the All-Star starting lineup at second base in 1965, in left field in 1973 and 1974, in right field in 1975, at third base in 1976 and 1978, and at first base in 1981 and 1982.

Edd Roush

THE ONLY PLAYER ever ejected from a game for falling asleep in the outfield.

Roush was wide awake enough to hit .323 in an 18-year career, get elected to the Hall of Fame in 1962, and live to the age of 94, but on June 8, 1920, he was thrown out of a game at the Polo Grounds in New York for falling asleep on the field. Playing center field for the Cincinnati Reds against the Giants, Roush became bored during a protracted argument involving Reds manager Pat Moran and the umpires over a call made at home plate. He lay down in the outfield, set his head on his glove, and soon was fast asleep. When play resumed, efforts to awaken him were not immediately successful. The umpires gave Roush an early shower for delay of game.

Chico Ruiz

THE ONLY MAJOR leaguer to pinch-hit for both Pete Rose and Johnny Bench.

Ruiz hit for Rose on July 26, 1964, in the eighth inning of a 7-2 rout of the Pittsburgh Pirates. On August 28, 1967; Ruiz pinch-hit for Bench in the ninth inning of Bench's major league debut. Bench had been retired three straight times, and Ruiz was to end the game against the Philadelphia Phillies with the tying run on second base.

Babe Ruth

THE ONLY PLAYER to pitch 14 innings in a World Series game.

Ruth started and completed the longest World Series game in history on October 9, 1916, in game two for the Boston Red Sox against the Brooklyn Dodgers. Ruth allowed only six hits and won 2-1. The Babe won all three of his World Series games as a pitcher and had a streak of 29 consecutive scoreless innings. As a hitter, Ruth played in 41 World Series games, had a .326 batting average, and 15 home runs. He is also the only player to hit three home runs in two World Series games, the first in 1926 and the second in 1928.

Kip Selbach

THE ONLY OUTFIELDER to commit five errors in one game.

Selbach became the only outfielder since 1900 to make five errors in a single game, on August 19, 1902, with the Baltimore Orioles in an 11-4 loss to the St. Louis Browns. He is also one of only five outfielders since 1900 to be charged with three errors in one inning. That happened when he was with the Washington Senators in a 7-4 loss to the New York Yankees on June 23, 1904. Less than two weeks later, the Senators traded Selbach to the Boston Red Sox in exchange for Bill O'Neill, who became the only modern shortstop to commit six errors in one game.

Hank Severeid

THE ONLY CATCHER to call pitches in no-hitters on consecutive days.

With the St. Louis Browns in 1917, Severeid was behind the plate when Ernie Koob no-hit the Chicago White Sox on May 5 and again a day later when Bob Groom stopped the White Sox without a hit in the second game of a double header. Despite being no-hit two days in a row, the White Sox won the American League pennant. The Browns wound up in seventh place, 43 games out of first.

Art Shamsky

THE ONLY PLAYER to hit three home runs in a game in which he was not in the starting lineup.

Shamsky turned in the most unusual three homer game in big league history while with the Cincinnati Reds on August 12, 1966. Playing against the Pittsburgh Pirates, he did not enter the game until the eighth inning as a defensive replacement in the outfield. His first homer, in the bottom of the eighth, put the Reds ahead 8-7. After a Pittsburgh comeback, Shamsky hit a second homer in the 10th to tie the score 9-9. A two-run homer in the 11th, Shamsky's third, tied the score again, at 11-11. The Pirates won the game 14-11 in 12 innings before Shamsky had a chance to bat again.

Ernie Shore

THE ONLY PITCHER credited with a perfect game in which he was not the starting pitcher.

Shore is the only relief pitcher credited with a no-hitter of any description. On June 23, 1917, Babe Ruth, the starting pitcher for the Boston Red Sox, was ejected for arguing a ball-four call to Washington Senators lead-off hitter Ray Morgan. Shore replaced Ruth on the mound and, due to the rules of the day, had to pitch without a warm-up. Morgan was thrown out by catcher Sam Agnew on a steal attempt. After Morgan was retired, Shore proceeded to mow down the next 26 Washington hitters to win 4-0. Shore's performance is classified in the record books as a perfect game.

Enos Slaughter

THE ONLY HALL of Famer with over 70 career pinch-hits.

More than 25 players in major league history have more career pinch-hits than Slaughter, but none are in the Hall of Fame because Cooperstown is reserved for every-day players. Slaughter was a regular out-fielder with the St. Louis Cardinals between 1938 and 1953, then spent six seasons as a part-time player with the New York Yan-kees, Kansas City Athletics, and Milwaukee Braves. During those six years, Slaughter collected 68 of his 77 pinch-hits. Next on the list of Hall of Fame pinch-hitters are Ernie Lombardi and Willie McCovey with 66 each.

Homer Smoot

THE ONLY PLAYER to hit into a quadruple play.

Playing for the St. Louis Cardinals against the New York Giants on July 1, 1903, Smoot hit a fly to Roger Bresnahan in center field with the bases loaded. Bresnahan threw to catcher John Warner to retire Clarence Currie trying to score from third for the second out. Warner then fired the ball to shortstop George Davis to nail Patsy Donovan attempting to advance from first for the third out. Even though the inning was over, Davis saw John Farrell, who started the play as the runner on second, trying to score and instinctively threw the ball home. Warner tagged Farrell for the "fourth out" of the inning.

Warren Spahn

THE ONLY PITCHER to lead a league in complete games seven years in a row.

This streak is all the more remarkable when one considers that it began in 1957 when Spahn was 36-years-old. Six years later, at the age of 42, he led the league by completing 22 of his 33 starts for a 23-7 record. During the seven consecutive years he led the league in complete games, he finished 145 of his 241 starts and had a 147-81 record, and topped the National League in victories five times, in innings pitched and shutouts twice each, and in earned run average and winning percentage once. Spahn ended his career in 1965 with 363 wins and was elected to the Hall of Fame in 1973.

Tris Speaker

THE ONLY PLAYER with more than 750 career doubles.

Considered by many to be the greatest center fielder of all time, Speaker set the all-time record for two-base hits with 793 between 1907 and 1928 with the Red Sox, Indians, Senators, and Athletics. Speaker also ranks fifth in base hits (3,515), sixth in triples (223), seventh in batting average (.344) and eighth in runs scored (1,881).

Casey Stengel

THE ONLY MANAGER to go 32 innings in one day without a win.

Stengel had many long days as manager of the New York Mets, but none more lengthy than May 31, 1964. In the longest double header in major league history by innings (32) and time (9 hours, 52 minutes), the Mets dropped a 5-3 decision to the San Francisco Giants in the regulation 9 innings and an 8-6 count in the 23-inning nightcap at Shea Stadium.

Stuffy Stirnweiss

THE ONLY PLAYER to win a batting championship and finish his career with an average under .270.

Stirnweiss is one of six Yankees with batting titles. The others—Babe Ruth, Lou Gehrig, Joe DiMaggio, Mickey Mantle, and Don Mattingly—are among the best players in baseball history, whereas Stirnweiss is barely known. In 1943 as a rookie, he hit only .219, but rose to .319 in 1944 and won the 1945 batting title with a .309 mark. Stirnweiss led the league in hits, stolen bases, runs scored, and triples in both 1944 and 1945. In 1946, when players in the service returned to civilian life, Stirnweiss was again an ordinary player, hitting only .251. His career ended in 1952 with a .268 average.

Milt Stock

THE ONLY PLAYER to collect four base hits four games in a row.

A third baseman with the Brooklyn Dodgers, Stock was unstoppable between June 30 and July 3, 1923, collecting four hits in four successive games during which he was 16-for-23. Stock hit .289 both during the 1923 season and in his 14-year big league career.

Dean Stone

THE ONLY PITCHER to win an All-Star Game without retiring a single batter.

As a representative of the Washington Senators, Stone was winner in 1954 in an 11-9 American League triumph. Stone came on in relief with two out in the eighth and the Nationals leading 9-8. On Stone's first pitch, Red Schoendienst tried to steal home and was out on Stone's throw to catcher Yogi Berra. The Americans scored three in the eighth to lead 11-9 and Virgil Trucks pitched the ninth. Being announced as the winning pitcher was a sensation Stone seldom experienced: in eight years with six clubs, he was 29-39.

Steve Stone

THE ONLY PITCHER to give up a home run to Duane Kuiper.

Kuiper holds the record for most at bats with only one home run, coming to bat 3,379 times officially between 1974 and 1985 with the Cleveland Indians and San Francisco Giants. The homer came on August 29, 1977, while Kuiper was with the Indians and Stone with the Chicago White Sox. The Indians won the game 9-2 in Cleveland.

Bill Stoneman

THE ONLY PITCHER to throw two no-hitters with a career winning percentage under .400.

There have been 25 pitchers with two career no-hitters, and Stoneman has the worst career record, 54-85. The first of Stoneman's no-hitters came on April 17, 1969, in only his fourth major league start and just the 10th game of the Montreal Expos franchise. Stoneman beat the Phillies 7-0 in Philadelphia. The second no-hitter occurred on October 2, 1972, at Jarry Park in Montreal, the first no-hitter pitched outside of the United States. In that one, Stoneman defeated the New York Mets 7-0.

Lou Stringer

THE ONLY SHORTSTOP to commit four errors in his first major league game.

Stringer debuted for the Cubs at shortstop on April 15, 1941, in an Opening Day game against the Pittsburgh Pirates. Although he made four errors, he hit a double and a single to contribute to a 7-4 Chicago win. This was not only Stringer's big league debut, but his first professional game at shortstop. He played only seven more games at shortstop in a career which lasted until 1950.

Dick Stuart

THE ONLY PLAYER to lead his league in errors at his position seven seasons in a row.

Debuting in 1958 with the Pittsburgh Pirates, Stuart finished the season with 16 errors in only 64 games at first base. He led the league seven consecutive years in miscues, five in the National League and two in the American. For six of those seven seasons, he led the majors. Continuing to commit errors throughout his career, Stuart earned the nickname "Dr. Strange-glove."

Jim Tabor

THE ONLY PLAYER to hit two grand slams and four total home runs in the same day.

Playing third base for the Boston Red Sox on July 4, 1939, against the Athletics in Philadelphia, Tabor homered in the first game of the holiday double header as the Red Sox won 17-7. He added more fireworks in the second game with three home runs, two of which were grand slams, as Boston was victorious 18-12. Tabor drove in 11 runs in the two games.

Zack Taylor

THE ONLY MANAGER to use nine pitchers in a nine-inning game.

With the St. Louis Browns on October 2, 1949, Taylor used nine pitchers, each for one inning, in a 4-3 loss to the Chicago White Sox. The pitchers were Ned Garver, Joe Ostrowski, Cliff Fannin, Karl Drews, Bill Kennedy, Al Papai, Red Embree, Dick Starr, and Tom Ferrick.

Gene Tenace

THE ONLY PLAYER to homer in each of his first two World Series at bats.

During the regular season, Tenace hit only .225 with five homers, and during the playoffs had only one single in 17 at bats. But as the Oakland A's starting catcher against the Cincinnati Reds in the 1972 World Series, Tenace hit a home run in his first at bat in the second inning of game one to give the A's a 2-0 lead. With the score tied 2-2 in the fifth, Tenace stunned the Riverfront Stadium crowd with another homer, and the A's won 3-2. In game four at Oakland, Tenace again homered and the A's won 3-2. In the fifth game, he hit a three-run homer, although the Reds came back to win 5-4.

Lee Thomas

THE ONLY PLAYER to collect nine base hits including multiple home runs in one day.

Of the 10 players in history who have collected nine base hits in one day, only Thomas hit more than one home run. Playing with the Los Angeles Angels on September 5, 1961, against the Kansas City Athletics, Thomas had four singles and a double in the first game, but the Angels lost 7-3. He hit three home runs, and added another single in the nightcap, but Los Angeles lost again, 13-12. As a rookie in 1961, Thomas had 24 homers and a .285 batting average.

Tom Trebelhorn

THE ONLY MANAGER to guide his club to winning and losing streaks of 12 or more games in the same season.

The 1987 Milwaukee Brewers started the season with 13 consecutive victories, to tie a major league record for most consecutive wins at the start of the season. Trebelhorn's Brewers nearly negated those victories with a 12-game losing streak that began on May 3. Milwaukee finished the year with a record of 91-71.

Hal Trosky

THE ONLY ROOKIE to hit more than 30 homers and collect more than 200 hits.

With the Cleveland Indians in 1934, at the tender age of 21, Trosky hit 35 homers, collected 206 hits, and hit .330 with 142 runs-batted-in. More spectacular seasons followed, and after the 1940 season, he already had 215 lifetime homers, more than Babe Ruth at the same age. Severe migraine headaches soon ended Trosky's career, however, and he played his last game in 1946.

Virgil Trucks

THE ONLY PITCHER to throw two no-hitters in a season in which he had a losing record.

Trucks is one of five pitchers who have had two no-hitters in a season, and the other four—Johnny Vander Meer, Allie Reynolds, Jim Maloney, and Nolan Ryan—combined to win 73 games and lose 43 in their double no-hit seasons. In 1952 Trucks tossed two no-hitters for the Detroit Tigers, but stumbled to a 5-19 record. The first no-hitter came on May 15 against the Washington Senators, the second on August 25 against the New York Yankees. Trucks won both by a 1-0 score.

Elmer Valo

THE ONLY PLAYER to play on two clubs that lost 20 games in a row.

Only nine clubs in history have lost 20 games in a row, and Valo played on two of them. He was an outfielder on the 1943 Philadelphia Athletics, losers of 20 in a row, and on the 1961 Philadelphia Phillies, with 23 consecutive defeats. Valo was in the majors from 1940 through 1961 and hit .282 in 1,806 games.

Johnny Vander Meer

THE ONLY PITCHER to throw back-to-back no-hitters.

In 1938 with the Cincinnati Reds, Vander Meer had just eight lifetime wins when he threw the first of the two no-hitters on June 11, a 3-0 triumph over the Boston Braves. His next start was four days later in the first night game ever played at Ebbets Field in Brooklyn and the first night game in the majors outside Cincinnati, where after-dark baseball began three years earlier. In the ninth inning Vander Meer walked the bases loaded with one out, but he pulled out his second no-hitter in a row for a 6-0 win. When his career ended in 1951, he had a 119-121 record.

Jack Wadsworth

THE ONLY PITCHER to allow 36 hits in a single game.

Pitching for Louisville against Philadelphia on August 17, 1894, Wadsworth allowed 36 hits in a 29-4 loss. Sam Thompson, a future Hall of Famer, collected six of the hits off Wadsworth and hit for the cycle. This apparently was not Wadsworth's only bad afternoon in the majors, judging from his 6-38 lifetime won-lost record and 6.58 earned run average.

Bill Wambsganss

THE ONLY PLAYER to pull off an unassisted triple play in a World Series game.

The only triple play in World Series history was accomplished by Cleveland Indians second baseman Bill Wambsganss in the fifth game of the 1920 series against the Brooklyn Dodgers. In the fifth inning, with Pete Kilduff on second base and Otto Miller on first, Clarence Mitchell hit a solid line drive over second base. Wambsganss made a leaping catch as Kilduff and Miller ran on the play. Wambsganss stepped on second to retire Kilduff and tagged Miller near the bag. The Indians went on to win the game 8-1 and capture the world championship two days later.

Piggy Ward

THE ONLY PLAYER to reach base eight times in a game in only eight plate appearances in a nine-inning game.

Playing for the Cincinnati Reds in a 30-12 thrashing of Louisville on June 18, 1893, Ward had two singles and five bases on balls, and was hit by a pitch. It was the only highlight of Ward's 221-game, six-year career spent with five different clubs.

Lon Warneke

THE ONLY INDIVIDUAL to both play and umpire in both a World Series and an All-Star Game.

Warneke was a player in the World Series with the Chicago Cubs in both 1932 and 1935 and was an umpire in the Fall Classic in 1954. He played in the All-Star Game in 1933, 1934, and 1936, and was chosen for the team in 1939 and 1941. He was an All-Star Game umpire in 1952. Warneke pitched a no-hitter for the St. Louis Cardinals in 1941, but missed a shot at umpiring in a no-hitter during his seven years as an arbiter in the National League. Warneke had a 193-121 career record with a 3.18 earned run average.

Earl Weaver

THE ONLY MANAGER with a 20-game winning pitcher on his club for 13 seasons in a row.

When Weaver took over the Orioles at the All-Star break in 1968, pitcher Dave McNally was 8-8. He finished with a 22-10 record, the first of 13 years that Weaver was the only modern manager with a 20-game winner. The winners included Jim Palmer (eight times), Dave McNally and Mike Cuellar (each with four), and Pat Dobson, Mike Torrez, Wayne Garland, Mike Flanagan, Steve Stone, and Scott McGregor (one each).

Earl Webb

THE ONLY PLAYER to collect over 65 doubles in a single season.

Webb's major league record of 67 doubles occurred in 1931 as an outfielder for the Red Sox. It certainly has to be considered a fluke, because Webb's next-best season in hitting two-baggers was 30 in 1930. He played a total of seven seasons in the majors with the New York Giants, Chicago Cubs, Boston Red Sox, Detroit Tigers, and Chicago White Sox, and batted .306.

Carl Weilman

THE ONLY PLAYER to strike out six times in succession in a single game.

A pitcher with the St. Louis Browns, Weilman took a half-dozen fruitless turns at bat on July 25, 1913, while facing strikeout king Walter Johnson. On the mound, Weilman battled Johnson and the Washington Senators before the contest was called by darkness after 15 innings with the score deadlocked 8-8. Weilman's strikeout spree contributed to another record, as Johnson struck out 15, the most ever by a relief pitcher, in 11 1/3 innings.

Mickey Welch

THE ONLY PITCHER to strike out
the first nine batters to face him.

Pitching for New York on August 28,
1884, Welch fanned the first nine
Cleveland hitters in order en route to a
10-2 win. Welch struck out 13 in the game.
He had a 311-207 career record and was
elected to the Hall of Fame in 1973.

Max West

THE ONLY PLAYER to hit a home run in his only All-Star Game plate appearance.

Although Boston Braves outfielder Max West batted .261 in 1940 with only seven home runs, he was the National League's starting right fielder. In the first inning, West hit a three-run homer off Red Ruffing to send the National League to a 4-0 win. West was out of the game in the second inning, however, when he ran into the right field wall chasing Luke Appling's fly ball.

Harry Wheeler

THE ONLY PLAYER to hit two triples in an extra inning.

A lifetime .228 hitter, Wheeler moved into an odd corner of baseball trivia in a game between Cincinnati and Baltimore on June 28, 1882. Will White of Cincinnati and Doc Landis of Baltimore both pitched shutouts through nine innings. Both allowed four runs in the 10th, then Landis gave up seven tallies in the 11th, paced by Wheeler's two triples, to give Cincinnati an 11-4 win.

Del Wilber

THE ONLY PLAYER to account for all of the runs in a 3-0 game with three home runs.

Wilber hit only 19 home runs in an eight-year career, but he specialized in hitting them in bunches. On August 27, 1951, Wilber hit three homers off Ken Raffensberger of the Cincinnati Reds in a 3-0 Philadelphia Phillies victory. In 1953 with the Red Sox, Wilber hit home runs in two consecutive pinch-hit appearances.

Hoyt Wilhelm

THE ONLY PLAYER who homered in his first major league at bat and played in over 1,000 games without hitting another one.

Nearly 60 players have hit home runs in their first at bat; 8 of them, like Wilhelm, were pitchers, and 11 never hit another home run. But none of those 11 played as long as Wilhelm. Wilhelm's big debut came on April 23, 1952, with the New York Giants. Wilhelm was also the winning pitcher in relief as the Giants triumphed 9-5 against the Boston Braves. Wilhelm finished his career in 1972 with a batting average of .088, but became the first relief pitcher ever elected to the Hall of Fame.

Kaiser Wilhelm

THE ONLY MANAGER to watch his club score 23 runs in a game and lose.

In the highest scoring game in major league history, Wilhelm's Philadelphia Phillies lost 26-23 to the Chicago Cubs at Wrigley Field on August 25, 1922. The Cubs scored once in the first, 10 times in the second, and 14 in the fourth inning to take a 25-6 lead. The Phillies nearly pulled the game out with eight runs in the eighth inning and six in the ninth. Just 17 days earlier, on August 8, Wilhelm became the only manager to watch his pitching staff allow 46 base hits in one day, as the Phillies dropped 19-8 and 7-3 decisions to the Pittsburgh Pirates.

Cy Williams

THE ONLY PLAYER to lead the
league in home runs at the age of 39.

Williams led the National League in
home runs in 1916 with the Chicago Cubs
and in 1920, 1923, and 1927 with the Philadelphia Phillies, the latter at the age of 39,
the oldest player ever to top a circuit in
homers. Williams closed his career in 1930
with 251 home runs, which at the time was
third on the all-time list behind only Babe
Ruth and Rogers Hornsby.

Ted Williams

THE ONLY PLAYER to reach base in 16 consecutive plate appearances.

From September 17 through September 23, 1957, Williams reached base safely in 16 consecutive plate appearances with the Boston Red Sox on two singles, four home runs, nine bases on balls, and one hit by a pitcher. The streak was stopped on September 24, when Hal Griggs of the Washington Senators induced Williams to ground out. Williams finished the season, at age 39, with a .388 average.

Hack Wilson

THE ONLY PLAYER whose home run production fell by over 40 from one season to the next.

Wilson hit a National League record 56 home runs in 1930 for the Chicago Cubs, but hit only 13 in 112 games in 1931. Also in 1930, Wilson set a major league mark with 190 runs-batted-in. That figure fell to 61 in 1931, and his batting average dropped from .356 to .261.

Owen Wilson

THE ONLY MAJOR leaguer with more than 35 triples in a single season.

Wilson hit a record 36 triples as an outfielder with the Pittsburgh Pirates in 1912 in a season in which he had 19 doubles and 11 home runs. His feat is one of baseball's oddities because Wilson never had more than 14 three-baggers in any of the other eight seasons in his big league career. And no one else since 1900 has had more than 26 triples in a season.

Wilbur Wood

THE ONLY PITCHER to save more than 20 games and win more than 20 games in consecutive seasons.

With the Chicago White Sox in 1970, Wood pitched 77 games in relief and had 21 saves, along with a 9-13 record. The next season, manager Chuck Tanner made Wood a starter, and he responded with 22 wins, 13 losses, and 7 shutouts.

Rudy York

THE ONLY PLAYER to hit 18 home runs in a single month.

As a rookie catcher–third baseman with the Detroit Tigers in August 1937, York hit 18 home runs in 30 games. Entering the month, he had played in only 49 major league games and had 12 homers in 173 at bats and a .249 career batting average. Given a chance as an everyday player for the first time, York hit .333 during that month, scored 28 runs, and drove in 50. Home runs number 17 and 18 came on August 31 off Pete Appleton of the Washington Senators in a 12-3 Tiger win.

Zip Zabel

THE ONLY RELIEF pitcher to hurl over 18 innings in one game.

Zabel completed the longest relief stint in history on June 17, 1915. Playing for the Chicago Cubs, Zabel relieved Bert Humphries with two out in the first inning and pitched 18 1/3 innings to finish the 19-inning encounter with the Brooklyn Dodgers. The Cubs won 4-3.